crazy love

poems

# Crazy Love

anthony petrosky

louisiana state university press
baton rouge
2003

cloth
12  11  10  09  08  07  06  05  04  03
5  4  3  2  1

paper
12  11  10  09  08  07  06  05  04  03
5  4  3  2  1

Designer: *Amanda McDonald Scallan*
Typeface: *Minion*
Printer and binder: *Thomson-Shore, Inc.*

Library of Congress Cataloging-in-Publication Data:

Petrosky, Tony.
  Crazy love : poems / Anthony Petrosky.
    p. cm.
  ISBN 0-8071-2895-3 (cloth : alk. paper) — ISBN 0-8071-2896-1 (pbk. : alk. paper)
  I. Title.
  PS3566.E858C73  2003
  811'.54—dc21                                        2003005110

The author gratefully acknowledges the editors of the following publications, in which some of the poems in this book have appeared previously, sometimes in slightly different form: *Acre* ("Crazy Love," "Soon Enough"); *DoubleTake* ("All of This"); *Georgia Review* ("All of This," "Casals"); *English Record* ("Another Theory," "Wide Clear Margins"); and *Hubbub* ("We Are Here").

Two poems, earlier versions of sections of "All of This," appeared originally in *Imported Breads: Literature of Cultural Exchange,* edited by Philip Sterling (Lanham, Md.: University Press of America, 2002). Versions and excerpts of "Soon Enough," "It is snow," and "Another Theory" appeared originally in "In(side) Out(ing)," in *Genre by Example: Writing What We Teach,* edited by David Starkey (Portsmouth, N.H.: Boynton/Cook–Heinemann, 2001).

Many thanks to David Bartholomae, Ellen Bishop, Tom Crawford, Linda Kucan, Ginette Delandshere, and Sandi Henschel for their readings of earlier versions of this book. Thanks also to Naomi Zigmond, who graciously offered me the use of her Woods Hole house at a time when I needed to complete these poems. Without her generosity and the space she gave me, I could not have finished this book.

This publication is supported in part by a grant from the
National Endowment for the Arts.

*Ellen Ellen Ellen*

With the past falling away as an acceleration of nerves thundering and shaking aims its aggregating force like the Metro towards a realm of encircling travel rending the sound of adventure and becoming ultimately local and intimate repeating the phrases of an old romance which is constantly renewed by the endless originality of human loss the air the stumbling quiet of breathing newly the heavens' stars all out we are all for the captured time of our being

FRANK O'HARA

# contents

# 1.

## Another Theory

Light muted rain
shapes a sycamore,
a maple gone red,
rows of high-rises
rising against the
gray, a dab of red
Hangul, a green
sign illuminated,
flashing to stop
then go, red to
yellow on black
macadam, both
sides outlined by a
languorous weave
of bodies in coats,
umbrellas up, a
few appearances
of oranges, blues,
even some ducks
flat against black
like hypotheses in
this sea of appear-
ances, God's ad-
versaries, in this
sooty air ablaze
with traffic,
radios, TVs, a
gray that dis-
appears into
glow like eye
into I or see
into be in a
pool of light
that illuminates
poinsettias in a
green plastic pot
on the sidewalk

next to a coil of
black tubes next
to a stack of straw
mats behind the
cart full of tiny
tangerines and an
old woman, a red
apron, two hands
wet with juice.

# THE 1965 RIVERSIDE PARK PHOTOGRAPH

*family . . . either we code it as a group of immediate allegiances or else we make it into a knot of conflicts and repressions. . . .*

Roland Barthes
Camera Lucida

Vince

wouldn't live in a city.
He loved cabbages, their greens and purples, their veins and weight,
as well as garlic, the elephantine bulbs, the eggplants and gourds,
even the river with its wretched rise up the mountain into the house.

  He's at the basement table,
a bowl of cucumbers in sour cream, another of steaming potatoes,
sprigs of parsley, a glass of beer. He's in the heady odors of cut hay,
in the rotten tomatoes, the fermenting peaches, his thick hands
at night in the light on a tree, his mother in a white chair,
father's at the table, legs crossed, suspenders undone,
as kids, of which I am one, run into the dark while Murphy
chain-smokes Salems as his accordion shuffles a little sobbing,
some melancholy like this into a small dance and sway
between a gray mountain and a black red-moonlit river.

Billy

took a
pipe in
a fight
after a
game at
the arena
that night
he put a
knife to a
kid's throat
until Ricky

pulled him
off then his
father put
him in a
school out-
side town
from which
he'd return
on holidays
head shaved
in a uniform
with medals
on a pocket
and a slight
twitch in his
face at times
in his lips or
eyes


## Annie

Carole got laid in the back while we drove around.
A guy I just met behind the wheel made jokes.
Carole said to "tell Annie we went to a movie."
Annie stared at me and said I was a lying little
prick. I don't know where she got her red hair.
She fried fish on Fridays, chicken on Mondays,
casseroles on Sundays. Laundry on Saturdays.
Frank put a pulley on the lines and scars on her
face. She put a boning knife into his shoulder.
He put her through a window. Barbara,
her youngest, went the next year to the nuns;
Carole had a girl she named Annie, then Frank
died a year later in a cave in. The air stunk.
Annie got rid of his beagles the next day. My
mother, her sister, commented on their absence
and the silence in the alley as if it was a creature

moved in to replace the dogs. Annie harbored her
bitterness in the small rooms of that flat filled with
knickknacks until her brother Mackey died, then
she let go of a torrent of tears that did not end, so
Barbara returned and Annie grew less coherent,
picking at her fingers then at her face until they bled
so much so that it was a relief to all, Barbara said, when
she died that June afternoon with a scream that laid out
        like the crack of a whip.


## Sonja

Imagine, she said, a bluesy man,
a brown-eyed, high-cheekboned man, a thin, smooth,
intense, always-at-attention, signaling man, a man-
cliché in the clouds in aluminum planes, a lying-
to-himself man, a man with his hands full on his
beltway, a leg man, an I-love-women man up
and down the coast, until his wife leaves, then he's
a heavy-scene man, the three kids lost in the shuffle,
in the divorce blur, the only people he's ever loved
for free because, you see, he's got it in his mind that
he's got to be out for himself, like a beacon or a light
in a tower, not to mention the dope, alcohol and sex
which are, he tells himself, pleasures he's earned,
everything is earned, it's always he deserves it,
he worked for it, it's never a giving over to anyone,
except the kids who save him from himself
by allowing him to make another self, but that's
a lot later, and for now,

                  he's on the edge, slipping
farther by the days into the dopey alcoholic sadness,
just like his father and his father's father, so he gets
close to a young woman in her twenties, full of life,
until her husband, a mainline Philly man the size of
a bear gets the drift and threatens to pull him apart,

but this lady moves out into a garret,
maybe she's taken with his lies,
maybe she's in love,
maybe she's looking for another life,
but the main man was born to be
unconscious, at least in this part of the story, so
he lays this trip on her (you've heard it all before)
having to do with finding himself, no promises,
but with the "I-think-I-love-you" talk, as he's thinking
to himself the "god-I-love-to-fuck-her" thoughts, but
he's on his way out of the country into anonymity
he'll imagine later as spiritual, a feeling of being connected
to everyone, except, of course, to himself or to the woman back
home, who is and isn't waiting as she's back in the sack with
her soon-to-be ex, although she was, as she said later, juggling
both of them, as he did earlier before he hit the mainland,
then got lost in the culture, only a little language by his side,
his buddy Jim holding him together, knotted up with desire,

                  then in an extended panic born from his finally
figuring out she was back in the sack with the bear, he, well he's
not sure what happened next, he flips out again, he can't sleep,
and when he does, he dreams about his mother, he remembers
her weeping, her naked once, bruised; he wrings his hands now
so much so that he notices himself in the company of others, as
he notices his kids creeping back into his daydreams, a jealousy
too having to do with the young woman sitting on the fence, fuck-
ing the Philly man, on top, or sucking on his dick, curled into him
  at night when the phone rings and rings, looking into the stories he
tells and the ones he might tell, as the tellers of the tale always have
the benefits of hindsight, foresight, predetermination
and prophecy,

            so he heads home, crying on
the plane, crying in her arms, getting-laid crying, holding-his-kids
crying, emptying-out-his-savings-account crying: he's a bluesy
man, he still thinks he can go it alone, but it's no secret anymore
that he can't and won't, though he'll get a schedule with his kids,
and she'll fight with him every inch of the way.

Clem Zickus,

                              a retired railroad man with a relentless
penchant for cards and craps, never mind his impossible
eyes encased in thick glass, had this habit of holding his

cards an inch away from each eye, one at a time, so that
his nose seemed to get in the way, then he'd thwack it
with his forefinger. His wife, Della, my mother's oldest

sister, a worry as thick as time, a scraped heart, fidgeted
while she sucked her teeth. "Just don't get loaded," she'd
say at Clem, "and fall all over everything." She drank tall

gin fizzes from my mother's frosted glasses and left her red
lipstick blurred on the gold edge. Her youngest, Tommy,
copy edited for the *Trib* and always sat on Clem's left when

he played, sipping his whiskey slow, a Pall Mall in a nonstop
chain of them dangling from his lip, his long fingers yellowed
and thin like my mother's. My father loved them all and what

they stood for. He'd work nights at Dalmatia's and haul home
the drunks to be ready when Clem appeared out of Chicago with
Bobby, his oldest, driving one of his new Caddies all night in an

insomnia to play those five or six days as they moved through
Illinois and New York, down into Pennsylvania and Virginia into
basements and kitchens like ours: their Joey Johns, their Annies

and Macken Spaces, their Whitey Fialkos. They are all gone
now with their hallucinations and victories, their cancers
and heart attacks, their rolled white sleeves and their ruby rings.

2.

Crazy Love

Rain rain
exploding in
a dream Ma
drove in silver

sheets though
she never could
a red Opal of all
things with me

into a wall from
which I woke
keening oh Ma
gone all these

years buckled to
beds shuffled to
beds and boards
always in need

of love though
you said yours
ran to us it was
dissolution that

washed through
when Ellen held
me under those
soaked sheets

## Soon Enough

December: no trees,
        no lights, no fights
for us. "Remember the Rizzleys?" Gina
        said from L.A. yesterday.
"Remember Mrs. Rizzley called
        and said Dad
        was passed
        out in the
        gutter in
        front of
        their house?
You and Ma had to go get him. I was so
        embarrassed.
        Mrs. Rizzley
        was my teacher."
        Okay,
how many of you remember shit like this? I
had forgotten the Rizzleys for forty years.
        *Fuck You Up:*
*Childhood Memories.* The book in which
        self-made victims
        and bystanders speak.
Who speaks for him or her?
Could it have been different?
        Why doubt it?
The poem doesn't bridge the gap.
It intrudes conflicting desires into
        the fog hanging over
        the fields of snow. Cold.
        Distant. Be
a bird, a crow, a jay; fly away dear
        heart to L.A. and stay
and stay in the pines, the lines and lines of
        traffic and coke. Snow
for a week. Do you miss the sun? Have you loved
        the frozen tops of houses?

It is snow now,

        tedious
White into which we
        go from
This room. White
        walls, gray
Floor. What would I
        give for
Blue? Blue blouse (who
        calls it that
Anymore) Ellen wore. A
        blue rug
At my father's funeral. Gone
        blue I was
For months and appear here
        again where I
Thought it would dissipate
        into you. And
You. Hyun Ock's blue hat. Ji Un's
        blue shirt. A
Bell. Six. Tell me what you believe
        we should do.
        Into the sky blue as it is,
Not the day this began, white streaked
        onto it, a disgruntled
Edge tore. Have you kept
        Your promises?
Not me. It was a week ago. Since
        then fourteen bus rides,
        seventeen meals, all with rice,
        love. That again. Is it
Possible to not be a cliché?
        Rain five days. Sun three.
        Two calls from the coast.
The dogs bark. Pink light. A green roof. I
        need some color. Why
Do you wear black all of the time? Even
        the orange barrels. Even

A red car. Even a yellow bus. Do
        you think in one gesture
We can see a person? Kyung Soon said so
        that night throwing
Her black hair to the side with a flip
        of her hand, then a turn
Towards Ellen. In one moment all
        moments. We've heard that
Before. Gestures open to private
        rituals. Movements. My father
        seldom looked up when he walked
In brown shoes, black laces, blue trousers.
We buried him in them in Buffalo
        which seems like a curse
Doesn't it? My mother in L.A. in the dirt.
        It gets into everything, Ellen
Said in Kwangju, in that apartment
        two years in construction.

In the bus with no

windows the bus with
three horns no empty seats
no discernible color old leather
canvas bamboo new plastic cases
tied with ropes on the top rack in
that bus to Dali the walled city to
the north city an emperor diverted
mountain streams under his roads his
granite so that he could share with his
people the sounds of the water itself in
pools in public places baths watering
troughs the emperor knew he would be
remembered for even as he grew old he
knew the virtues of granite his three guides
his treasures as he called them in the old
tradition of simplicity patience compassion
return is the movement he knew yielding
the way one day the stone dissolves
the streams return soft overcomes
hard but for now this would be his
accomplishment like these walls
through which the bus to Dali passes
water buffalo wooden carts the rice
green as far as he could see to the bare
treeless mountains the wood gone even
before his time the lake shimmering at
its base the boats hauling nets the fish
scarce he imagined a hatchery surrounded
by nets he built it posted guards to help
the disbelievers until the fish multiplied
it took how many years to convince everyone
three to put fish in their bowls with rice
from the same fields the bus to Dali passes
on the berms the emperor had built
to hold the water to move the people
nine hundred years later the stones still
slowly dissolving the water still moving

under the streets his hatchery still fenced
with nylon nets now the mountains bare
in the clouds tonight the full moon's jagged
light breaks through the people on the bus
to Dali eleven hours out of Kunming we can
see the walls but no buildings rise above them
the emperor knew to keep close to the ground
to use everything without destroying it the way
trees were taken for firewood he understood
the recklessness of desire the nearsightedness
of need so he left one side the south side of
the mountain bare so the lesson of the trees
would not be forgotten he had the trees the
sycamores the ginkgoes the cedar cultivated
replanted then ordered sod cut dried
burned to save trees he burned manure
with straw he did this the chronicles told
nothing held him captive his own house
he kept small bare in his desire to return
as he does now thousands of seasons later
in a teller of a tale a woman creased by sun
time children many times she says the markets
throb with entrepreneurs no sense everything
their desire TVs cars western clothes lies she jabs
her hands hands ragged with soil with cracks
lies she gestures towards the front of the bus
the windshield cracked like a map the chuckle
of men drinking plum wine untying their knots
chewing hemp which the emperor grew to
sell to the Bai in the market he kept outside
the walls

In a narrow room

at the top of a hill
among the roofs
and branches, the
cantilevers and
hip walls, with
photographs here
and there, Patricia's
hands holding Ben's
small body, his blurred
hand reaching, his
round face harboring
a hint of my mother's,
as Matthew, maybe
three, sits on a beach
in a backwash of a white
shirt, and in another
both of them dance
on the porch of the old
house we loved, Ben
with his thumbs in his
ears, waving his hands,
me behind the camera,
Matt's hands moving
frenetically, the front
door open through
the screen and the
doorway beyond that
to the hall where we
hung photographs
of the friends and
relatives we arranged
ourselves among when
we had no idea of
the insults we would
trade years later in
the same hall when
we had little to do

with compassion
or the intricate
recognitions of what
we had become to
each other, saturated
as we were in every
argument on what we
had taken for love or
from each other or
others, the failures
of memory in the heat
of it all concealing us,
the births of our sons
in that white room,
the wet warm mass
of each one in turn
in the years in-between.

## In a slight sedimentation of things said

that summer that proposed instead a distant location
as distinct and describable as the back of her lover's
hand or palm turned in the thick air upward to
touch her face in a gesture even across the distance
between spring's and autumn's greens and reds gone
to gold in her photographs of her in the mountains

with that longing to be closer to be intimate thick as
humidity packed in a heavy space with various
others lingering as they pass on the streets in roars
of exhaust the buses trailing each other west
into the heartland where she consumed herself

with a lover who couldn't yet bring herself forward
from the heady altitude the discontinuity
not even knowing which sadness it was coming or
going between them the discrete feelings
associated with imminent change seasons with
places and lives temporarily disjointed yet

not quite a change she said a layering onto layers
already in place in the intimacies spoken through
such things as long letters involved conversations
revealing desires kept private out of a combination
of fears doubts desires so strong as not to be doubted
a tough place to be when you know better she said

over the black metal table iced coffee outdoors
twice then a third time drifting leaves catching her
eyes now and then in the busy street in a summer
that wouldn't be forgotten simply because she was
far away and talk was occasionally enough to keep
a connection as she said as precious as possible now

In Sophia

the trolleys' clack clack clack hiss precious electricity
In Sophia: sausages, schopska salads, the bleak
Sophia, streetlights dim, bare-bones electricity & water
& telephones, the infrastructure, as we say, the plumbing
& etc., etc. from the '30s &

something to drink
bira
lukewarm

Nietzsche loves to eat here with Proust on Tolbulchin
in the nameless restaurant in the dimness and smoke,
unnerved through the representations of time,
contesting life right back to its lack of sense.

colors, please oh please

The gray buildings & clothes
dark dark except for the red & green & yellow trolleys
& gold sparks of course.

Good old dour Nietzsche.
One of the *opposite men:*
*conscience . . . enhanced,*
*an unconditional*
*power-will.*

bread
goulash

*Moral evolution,* Proust whispers across the table.
*Danger in the alley and heart.*

horseradish
more bira

Nietzsche nods
and picks at the bread.

Proust sighs.

The trees grow distant shaking their arms.
The birds disappear and all the creatures
fold up into the magician's books.

*And as for happiness,* Proust broke in,
*it has almost a single usefulness—*
*to make unhappiness possible.*

*Suffering almost all the more deeply hollows out the heart.*

Almost.

It was late.
The sounds of silverware brought us around. The din.
Voices.
Gypsies begging.

In the closing moments, in the sweeping clear of the tables,
Proust said *love is a token of grief,* and Nietzsche announced
that even the best Will
                        is immaterial.
*A wave,* he motioned,
        *lost among waves.*

*And where do those waves of everything which is great and sublime*
        *finally flow out?*
*Isn't there an ocean for those torrents?*

We saw him in the park.

"Listen," he said, poking his bent, yellow
finger at the kid's round face, "don't

get anything you can't kill
when you're sick of it,"

which brought the other old men loosely
gathered around him to laugh cackling

dry sounds and nod in unison as if their strings
had been pulled at once, and the kid,

well, the kid, he didn't seem to get it,
not that he couldn't understand what was

said, no that wasn't it, he got that all right,
it was the abject, the cynicism that went by him,

the swirling blizzards of the ages, the resolutions
in God's name, no, it was the backwaters and discharges,

the deceitful little cocksuckers, it was that lineage that
went right by him in those limousines of fetid breath

as he turned to look up—
that's what he missed completely.

In Seoul in August we move slow

in a claustrophobia of humidity, cars, people
as thick as particulates in the parks and palaces

where ornately painted dragons float past heavenly
monks in a beyond copied from dreams then bombed when

Kim Il Sung convinced Mao with Stalin's magnanimously
self-serving blessing to hallucinate with him into a war in

which a fifty-caliber shell ricocheted into my uncle's head
and left him with thousands of others to be ploughed under

there, here where they worship the dead in manicured tombs
laced through the reforested hills in ritual devotion mainly to

the men who live built into Confucian doctrine and codes of public display,
politeness and deference fueling now a seemingly endless net of corruption

in which high-rises rise in rows in a haze of military fears, which hang like oil
in the air while the North starves itself into bizarre postures accompanied by

arrogance, that old cover, face-saving no matter what, about which we relent-
lessly complain, so even a small social act such as a dinner and a chat runs in

labyrinthine indirectness—my God it drives us crazy, always outside, always
incapable, so we turn to each other in prolonged glimpses of what we take

to be our selves in narrow streets lit with neon Hangul in fantastic colors
we can barely read but from which we take pleasure.

## Wide Clear Margins

oh
to be
in that
light,

the light
of this mid-
morning autumn
light, this morning
with death, your death,
a possibility surfaced in
the light intensely recogniz-
able, an obsession in the light
of a week, or was it two, gone by in
the gray light drowned in bric-a-brac,
in work, in the other obsessions, in the
saturation of it gone finally in the quick
decision of an observation, an examination,
the dread of every one from every year gone
again in this fucking wonderful light but not
without the trace of it, the anxiety, the possibility
of return, even after the incision, the laser cut with,
as he said, wide clear margins

oh to be in the light, the light of this
midmorning mindless autumn light, wigging in and out,
beginning again in the shadows of the light from the window
now on the sheets,
                    to be in love with you in the light beginning
again this mindless midmorning autumn.

My mother's most feminine of gestures,

      her presence in my hands,
           shapes this white space,
               the self of my-mother-myself,

slightly manic     jumpy,
      fashions surfaces like this
          with her long bony hands,
             shaping words *to be held*

in a vision of
winter that
stretches
before us of
you holding
me in the low-
lying fog that
ran the length
of the road and
the width of a
field covered
with snow
in our lights
near the sea

whose roar rose over the edge of the mezzotint
brackish green
hill
holding us
in place holding
each other

as we have been held

on days like this,
the light-shifting lull,
the birds chirring,
looking so not quite with-it
at their posts in the hemlocks

3.

# We Are Here

*Our ties to beings and things are so fragile they often break without our noticing.*

Edmond Jabes

In July and August at Murphy's place
      on the lake, dear
Bald, blue-eyed, bowlegged, sweet
      chain-smoking
Murphy, who said her good-byes on her way out
      the door for surgery
With no intention of returning, yet she did, thank God,
      in whom, by the way,
She said to say, she does not believe, though today,
      the anniversary
Of her resurgence, the wind has suddenly died, but sorry,
      there won't be a funeral
Here, although the fog arrived overnight, shifting in
      sheets across the water,
As uncertain as I was when the sun came up
      and I was the fog
As I treaded water, then lifted over the trees as
      one of the mysteries of this
Green and silver kingdom. That was this morning,
      but it didn't last,
Little does, and I like to complain as much as I love this
      place and the city
Displaced into memories. Who will speak kindly of you
      when you're gone?
Lying on the sofa in the afternoon heat,
      Fred, my friend Fred
Is headed for a splat like an egg on a flat rock
      on a manic binge. It's impossible
To talk an alcoholic out of drinking. Fishy
      Fred, crocked
To the gills. His hands shake. He repeats
      himself. Himself
A source of kindness I love. I waste
      my time worrying. It is
The end of July, which is not

A flowering month, although a stunning purple Iris
        bloomed in the bed
When we arrived. I should have taken its picture lit
        in early light. Let's see,
Ellen laughed, if we can be that beautiful.
        We weren't,
But the nasturtiums tasted deliciously peppery in an orange
        swirl, although Jane, Ellen's
New friend darted neurotically around the kitchen
        as her husband demonstrated
Himself into the center of attention even to the dismay
        of his kids who asked to be
Included in the sail he took in the outrageous wind
        that blew the clouds out
To sea. "Sugar comes to the sweetest," he said to Eric.
        His voice inserted like a needle
Into the kid who folded up in the striped chair on the deck
        with the wind blowing through
His lovely brown hair. "Why should it be so difficult
        to have wanted to be
Loved?" my sister asked on the phone in the sun.
        I was sweating
Rivers. "I would like to kill myself," Ma went on, "I'm
        so tired of this boring life,
But the ocean is too far, and I don't have a bus schedule." Oh Ma.
        "Tony, listen carefully:
Can you send me eight hundred bucks right away?"
        In photographs her smiles are forced. Pain
And alcoholics ruined her, so she continues in and out of hospitals
        on the coast in drizzle
Today, she said. "How are the kids, Tony? Do they remember
        me?" I remember Ma
In the heavy odors of fish frying, men whirling in smoke, Ma
        holding on to a glass
With both hands, in no one's hands now in a room in a glare
        in the windows. I wish
I were a better son. Today is better than yesterday. The wind
        has shifted, the fog
Has retreated to Little Bird Mountain. It is Wednesday, quiet
        and warm. Ellen

Is asleep, curled under the covers, her hands open at her sides.
		Open Ellen.
One white star hangs back in the window above
		the house on the hill lit
With two lights, the early light spilling in over her,
		her legs spread out across
The blue sheets like a pale sky holding not even a single plane
		or bird, only the white star
Which is her, of course, as corny as it sounds, as the kids
		rubbed their eyes and hair,
While I stood there in the kitchen with a coffee cup, a dream
		of love, desperate to hold it,
While the huge green moth with orange antennae clung perfectly
		still to the windowsill
Of the window to the lake, of what we have been looking for
		all year. We brought
Some kind of crazy desire here to see what had become muted
		between us, a longing
For tenderness, for each other's touch. How can a simple thing
		be so complicated? My
There's a lot of activity at the brown cottage. Maybe they also
		have come for love,
Banging their boats against the float.
		I wish we didn't have a phone.
		It was my father again.
		He wants. He wants
		this time to be buried
		in a mausoleum. Did
		I forget? It's already
		paid for, his voice
		repeats, stuck in
		ongoing, planning
		still, looking over
		his shoulder at
		the dirt. Seven
		thousand five
		hundred, the voice
		crackling on the line
		says, another grand
		for the reception,

the house goes to
Gina. He doesn't
approve of her
in Singapore or
with a man. The
father thinned
out to a voice
despondent
wants this taken
care of. The papers
are on the dining
room table.
Okay. Yes, I love you. Good-bye. I
would like to turn off
The phone. The kids wouldn't have any part of it.
They get calls every hour
from Eliza and Alexia: "helloisMattthere?" This gray day
I can hear the cars on
The road across the lake. I wish the wind would do something
about it soon, be a harbinger
Of daydreams, a spicy aroma, like the dried lavender
Kathryn sent. The kids
Chatter over pancakes. Ellen has turned toward the window
facing a row of pines
She loves. Some sadness haunts us. I'm "Mr. Narcissism."
*I'm Mr. Blue—*
*Woooo woo woo—*
*I'm worse to get rid of than a tattoo.*
What passes for intimacy passes
Into silence against a background of children and birds
in every windless tree. See,
A light drizzle has begun. The leaves are glassy-eyed,
restless. Ellen
Reclined on a bed in a cavernous room
lit with blue or green
Light, with unfamiliar women and her lover,
a woman with hazel eyes,
Spilling into her. She woke staring at the lake,
the moon in clouds, sliding
Comfortably onto me, into it in three seconds flat.

The roof leaked. The water
Stained the photographs of organs, stereometric columns,
        slender tubes of silver
Against white walls, the books lined up from Balzac to Tolstoy
        are also wet. I can see
An oval gold mirror, a small wooden sailboat hanging from the ceiling,
A bleached white skull of a steer above the mantel, old medical books,
A row of *Life* from the '50s, four spindle-back chairs, a tall mahogany
Victoria, rows of 78 records and blue glazed bowls filled with marbles.
        The rain has quit.
It lost interest. There's a slight breeze in the tops of the trees. What is
        so striking to remember?
The kids' faces. Our felicitous fall. The loons' calls.
        Too much coffee
Isn't the answer. I have the jitters. I didn't sleep well. The sun
        seethes into the room
I am in upstairs. Waves of heat cascade over the copper roof.
        Three ducks and our neighbors
Float past. We cannot live the way we want. Today,
        Friday, we have turned each other
Into stories. Whiny. Resentful. What can we do?
        Where can we go?
It's better to be bored than to argue.
        Here comes the sun.
A good night's sleep does wonders. We were together
        all day after
Intermittent clouds against a plane of solid blue,
        as we headed out
At first on the lumpy corduroy sofa. We were great.
        Desire keeps us
Afloat a lot. The geese hit the water
        in a wedge. They desire
Handouts. And I held on, trying
        not to disappear
Though I did. I was in charge of lunch so I had
        to go to Shaw's
In Rockland. I bought ham and cheese from Betty, Bing cherries
        from Montana, champagne
For Ellen, Honey Grahams for the kids, lettuce and celery, a pepper.
        It was weird

And crowded. An old man in a yellow jacket followed me, insisting
       loudly that he knew
I was CIA or FBI, and "God bless you," he said next to the bread. I
       thought it must be
My aviators from the J. Peterman Company. I've been a fraud before
       though. I rowed across the lake
With the Muslims dying in the Balkans and almost lost two bags of
       groceries in the waves. I wasn't watching.
What is going on in the world? It is so depressing.
I have finished another novel. "So long, Señor Maioranos. Nice
       to have known you—
However briefly." Who feels like writing?
       Not me.
The kids' metal music clatters in the living room. The place
       is closing in.
       Mayday. SOS.
       Over and out.
             This morning's smatter-
             ing of sun has taken
             up in the small clearing
             as the light builds to
             white. Today
More fragmented than usual.
       Tomorrow it'll be gone.
Time flies: Sigourney Weaver and I
       will never meet. Unrequited
Everything. She's stunning in these Mapplethorpe
       photographs. Cindy Lauper looks
Tough. Grace Jones: such a mesmerizing stare. And Susan
       Sarandon in a sheet, let's
       have coffee and a chat. No letters
In a month. Rain explodes.
       It was the phone. Looking haggard,
July is done.
       "Gina for you," Ellen says.
       "Ma's bad. You should come."


           She ate
the yellow pears slice by
slice, the juice on her

lips. No one had
cleaned her teeth; we
brushed her hair; "She
recognizes you," Gina
said.

                    In Shanghai
When the call came it was July, the heat hung in the room,
            the black phone hissed. She had
Been gone a decade and I didn't have a clue
            she had a place inside of me
            with gold drapes, doilies
            under vases, angels arranged
            in swirls of cigarette smoke,
Betty's and Rosie's voices—
            "Come on, Bernice.
            Wake up, Bernice."
We flew the great arc; the sheets of white turned
            to green, then we landed
years ago. Today,
fogophobia.
No patience.
Here comes that big
white Bayliner with
the blue stripe again.
And the sun finally.
Seas three feet every
four seconds. Winds
of 34 knots or greater
not expected. Too
bad. Bar Harbor,
which we never visit,
can expect traffic jams
out to the Hague line.
Not General Haig,
right? Another imagin-
ary line. Ellen wants to
know if this is a poem
or a shopping list. "I'm
not reading it," she says.
Okay, then it's a poem. A

brown spider the size of a
quarter repairs its web
over the kitchen window.
It works fast cultivating
insignificance. Who isn't?
Let's not get into that.
Gray day. The weather
forecast is from Gray,
Maine. Who is that kid
screaming in the water
worse than a radio?
Two boys paddle on
a surfboard. Visibility
variable: below a mile in fog.
Naked Ellen types at the
picnic table. Beads of sweat
run down her side to the
bench which is now damp.
Writing is her accomplice.

4.

## All of This

*All of this fleeting world:*
*A star at dawn, a bubble in a stream;*
*A flash of lightning in a summer cloud,*
*A flickering lamp, a phantom, and a dream.*

*The* Diamond Sutra

## 1.

I feel like I'm locked inside of myself.
Maybe love will open the door,
maybe I just don't have the right words yet.
Maybe I'm stuck in Hollywood's versions of love.
Maybe my head is full of nonsense. Or maybe
I'm stuck in symbolism. You know, what love stands for.
Love of another represents self-love, and self-love, or any love, isn't
possible, as Graham Greene, that depressive, said, without love of God.
Or maybe I'm stuck because I'm trying to put God and love together
like Simone Weil, mystically out of her mind, soaring
through the tiny blue flowers in the wild vetch,
telling her story of two prisoners separated by a wall,
tapping messages to each other, the wall at once their separation
and communication, so that the wall is like God, and that is
what we have to learn to love. She suffered relentlessly,
like my father who can't move anymore, who has given up
the idea of time in a chair in front of the TV,
and my mother in a nursing home with her seven strokes.
I want to stop now and think about their suffering,
as if they belonged together like a Christmas cactus and its pink blossoms.
I want to send them all the sweetness they can hold in their arms.
I want their grief to matter. And I want God to remember them,
to make up for all of this in a sweeping gesture of mercy
            like a warm rain.

So I am praying for harmony, for kindness,
for an annihilation of suffering; I am praying,
even though I should know better, for love
and desire. Voracious desire, I told Ellen once.
I wanted her, like that word, *voracious*.
I couldn't think of anything else;
I annihilated everything, even the broken furniture
in the purple loosestrife along the tracks, in my obsession,
and I thought I was entering paradise. When it was over,
when we folded our wings back without flinching, when we
made tea and whispered the words, I love you, it took eight
more years. It was almost impossible even with all the rain

and good done on earth, even with all the suffering, with
the words and singing and touching, even
with all the little miracles.

#

Here's some pale ochre lilies tethered to white threads
in a frenzy
in the concrete pool.

Here's some old mothers in a blur of glass,
pink sweaters,
blue rubber slippers,
flowered housecoats.

Here's bedpans,
sour air,

a nurse,
a white doorway,

Ma's shut eyes.
Her gray head slumped over the chair.
Her curled hands.
Some dried mint in her paper cup.
A daisy in her bowl.

Too green pines.
A gaudy sun.

#

Gray and calm. Mist. Mosquitoes
languidly drift in. A crow. My sister in from the coast
with her son, her swallow. A solitary
osprey glides out over the water. Here
wind gusts in elegant ripples. God-the-Wind

graces thermals and updrafts that waft the kids' voices in
then out like Ma's tinny radio.

Now the water looks like a dark cloth, six hundred acres sewn
with tiny insects. What a way to live. One thing or another always
coming up from under. Thunder in the distance.

2.

Kwangju.
Two A.M.
The phone.

Barely a whisper says
to me he loves me

then fades,

incomprehensible

broken open
heart—

he calls me.
And we cry.

Steve said he took his hand, more like a claw than a hand,
        to pull him up.

"I just wanted to thank you," my father told him, "for being my friend.
        I'm going to die."

#

Cry and cry and cry.

Maybe you already know how sorrow seeps from the sky then
runs into our arms and faces, the way it moves like an old affliction
with remorse or regret

into all that's left—

three wooden rosaries naproxen celebrex tolmetin pennies
shoes dishes in the sink the kids' photographs    my head hurts
it's his palms on my back
his all-eyes emaciated face—

Maybe you already know you must do something

so furtive
while the rain falls
lightning falls

then you're in the river
voices build and break
and nothing changes yet everything changes

then the sun is remarkable finally
and burns us so in love with it
and warms the waters
and we feel again heat in each other
as Cypriot children dance a Hora
and mercy is in short supply in Kosovo
and between us there are only these words
and a radio on a window ledge outside the Jing Jang that plays Hayden all night
as 747s land while the sun comes up in Madrid as hundreds of thousands
of faucets run and toilets flush and faces get shaved and love gets made
and the children sleep as the dogs pace in a slight wind that ripples the maples.

3.

That night my son woke bolt
upright into the steady sound

of a heavy rain in a wind tossing
cans and branches into the streets

the sensation of the dream of being
lifted into a visible ecstatic electric

cloud above a green green field
caused him to shiver to hold him-

self saturated still in that current
lifting his body while he stared

amazed at his hands and legs and
his wrists along which traveled a

stream of layered colors of blue
red and silver shapes changing

to first the body of a bear then a
head of a man then simply a line

of silver snapping like a whip
along his fingers until he woke

suddenly staring at his hands
and shivering in the sounds of

the rain outside and a voice not
unlike my father's calling him

back to that place where he was
not able to go then or since then

#

                    I dreamt
                    he woke through the drone
                    and we could hear Casals crying

then in the Sarabande of the last suite, a voice told us
to go for a walk, so we closed our eyes and went into the park
luminous with light with Ben who plays as if he's possessed,
whose enormous feet kept us planted to the ground as we took
the steep path down to the river while we held hands, the heat
from our fingers moving up through our arms as we crossed
over the fallen trees washing themselves like prehistoric centipedes
in the currents near the shore while we pulled each other along over
the rocks and trees towards a spillway, towards Casals playing
all alone for the embankments and the burnt out ragweed for
the weepy slates and pines.

                              #


Here he comes again

caught like a twig in the wind,

his bent, twisted hands,
his rotten knees and shoulders,
his disintegrated hips.

He has cut holes in his shoes to let his bones through.

He loves this austerity.

## 4.

Gone completely silver now,
watching from a distance as she always did,
Ma steps out of that wind into substance with the sun
behind her so that she is all shadow, yet I can see
she carries an apron full of mushrooms as she often
carried greens or corn or beans in those days.

"You remember, Tony," she says in the breeze,
"it was the summer we moved."

She was her worries and her molds,
her crumbling limestone.

She was rain and rheum and soaked sheets.
She was nausea and vomiting,

and hands full of hair
in her roses and wisteria,

and when she died in the stems and scree,
she resembled someone resembling grief resembling rage.

#

She comes and goes     sodden woods seep
into greens and blacks     an open window     another
floats by     she's at the curtains     her long fingers repose
with a smoke at a table     her hair in curlers     she rants
at the trees and sky     she warbles     who returns her crazy love
who are the trees     the saints in white shirts on the line     our father
waves bread across the table     sips coffee     purses his lips     sighs
sunrise     put spite in their eyes     and winds
out of the west     in this     another tumultuous day
in an unimaginable series     as the light has now shown the trees
to be swaying     changing their greens in this light *breeze*
a word she liked and used often     *don't worry dear*
*it will be a breeze*

5.

A thin green sheen
of pollen comes in

from the windows
on the table, chairs,

the ratty sofa and
rug, plant dust,

spring showing
its colors barely

visible, except in the
right slant of light,

spores in the nooks
and crannies preparing

to turn the inside
out with a little rain,

a leak in a roof, a
window, a rotten

slice of wood, a
sill, a damp carpet,

plaster dusted to
dust onto us.

*

My people who
lived here loved

anger and tenderness
simultaneously and

were always broke
or drunk or both

and quite beautiful
as I remember them

in their inconsolable
sadness and fear in

this pale blue room
with the still cracked

windows where we
have seen them

off, one by one,
each in time,

with a touch of
hands, a brush of

lips, good-bye,
have a nice trip.

# notes

In Kwangju, the Korean city in the south of the peninsula, the students and workers opposed the government in 1980 in a revolution in the streets that led to confrontations with the Korean military and the Kwangju Massacre, in which thousands of people were hunted down and killed.

Hangul, the Korean language, in its written form is quite different from Chinese and Japanese, and when shaped into neon tubes and lit, it is at times beautiful.

Dali, a small town near Kunming and the Chinese border with Myanmar, is home to a number of Chinese native minorities, including the Bai, whose stunning artistic designs are hardly known, even in China.

"In Sophia" is for Linda Kucaw.

"Wide Clear Margins" is for Ellen Bishop.

"We Are Here," dedicated to the memory of James Schuyler, occasionally uses lines or phrases of his which are sometimes rewritten and borrows lines as well from Tom Waits.

"All of This" is for my sons, Matthew and Benjamin, in memory of my parents.